Date: 8/31/15

BACKYARD ANIMALS
RACCOONS

by Kristin Petrie

Checkerboard
Library

An Imprint of Abdo Publishing
www.abdopublishing.com

www.abdopublishing.com

Published by Abdo Publishing, a division of ABDO, PO Box 398166, Minneapolis, Minnesota 55439.
Copyright © 2015 by Abdo Consulting Group, Inc. International copyrights reserved in all countries. No part of this
book may be reproduced in any form without written permission from the publisher. Checkerboard Library™ is a
trademark and logo of Abdo Publishing.

Printed in the United States of America, North Mankato, Minnesota.
102014
012015

 **THIS BOOK CONTAINS
RECYCLED MATERIALS**

Cover Photos: iStockphoto
Interior Photos: Alamy p. 21; AP Images p. 27; Glow Images pp. 5, 8, 18, 20, 22; iStockphoto pp. 11, 12, 13,
    14, 17, 29; MARTIN WOIKE/FOTO NATURA/MINDEN PICTURES/National Geographic Creative p. 1; PHIL
    SCHERMEISTER/National Geographic Creative p. 10; Science Source pp. 15, 19, 24–25; Superstock p. 23

Series Coordinator: Megan M. Gunderson
Editors: Tamara L. Britton, Bridget O'Brien
Art Direction: Neil Klinepier

Library of Congress Cataloging-in-Publication Data

Petrie, Kristin, 1970- author.
  Raccoons / Kristin Petrie.
      pages cm. -- (Backyard animals)
  Audience: Ages 8-12.
  Includes index.
  ISBN 978-1-62403-662-0
1. Raccoon--Juvenile literature. I. Title.
  QL737.C26P485 2015
  599.76'32--dc23
                              2014024636

TABLE OF CONTENTS

RACCOONS

What animal wears a black mask and has rings on its tail? This creature also has fingerlike toes. Sometimes this animal looks like it is washing its food, but it also eats garbage! Lastly, this animal seems to waddle when it walks, but it climbs with great skill.

What is this strange and interesting creature? It is the raccoon! Raccoons are mammals from the scientific family Procyonidae and the genus *Procyon*. The northern raccoon's scientific name is *Procyon lotor*. It is also called the North American raccoon and the common raccoon. The crab-eating raccoon is another well-known species. Its scientific name is *Procyon cancrivorus*.

Common raccoons are frequent visitors to campsites, city parks, and of course, backyards. They are curious and intelligent animals, making them both entertaining and mischievous. Keep reading to learn more fascinating facts about raccoons!

SCIENTIFIC CLASSIFICATION

Kingdom: Animalia
Phylum: Chordata
Class: Mammalia
Order: Carnivora
Family: Procyonidae
Genus: *Procyon*

The raccoon genus's name, *Procyon*, means "before" and "dog" because raccoons were believed to come from the same ancestor as dogs. The word *lotor* means "washer" because raccoons were once believed to wash their food before eating it.

WHAT'S IN A NAME?

The word *raccoon* comes from an Algonkian word, *arathcone*. It means "least like a fox" or "he scratches with his hands."

ORIGIN & HABITAT

Where did raccoons come from? Raccoons, bears, and pandas shared an ancestor 30 to 40 million years ago. Raccoons are native to North America. Over time, the many raccoon species we know today **evolved** and spread across the Americas.

Today, raccoons inhabit a large geographical range. For example, the northern raccoon is found throughout southern Canada. Its range covers all of the United States except for parts of the Rocky Mountains. The northern raccoon also lives throughout Mexico and south into Central America.

The crab-eating raccoon's range overlaps with the northern species in Central America. More of these raccoons are found in forests and along coastlines in South America.

Other less common species are found on tropical islands in the Caribbean Sea. For example the pygmy, or Cozumel, raccoon lives on the island of Cozumel off Mexico.
It is critically **endangered**.

IT'S ALL RELATIVE
Raccoons share the family Procyonidae with olingos, coatis, and kinkajous.

Canada

United States

Mexico

Where Northern Raccoons Live

N

North America

South America

Europe

Asia

Africa

Australia

Members of the raccoon family have also found a home in the Eastern **Hemisphere**. Raccoons were first introduced in Europe and Asia in the 1900s. They currently have strong populations in countries such as Germany, France, Great Britain, the Netherlands, Russia, and Japan. In many areas, they are considered a **nuisance**.

Within its **habitat** and region, the raccoon has a home range in which it remains. Home ranges vary greatly in size. They can measure 100 to 250 acres (40 to 100 ha). In **urban** areas, a home range may be just 1 mile (2.5 km) across. The size of this area depends on how much food is available.

Den location also helps determine a raccoon's home range. Raccoons prefer damp, wooded spots for denning. These conditions provide protection, food, and water. Dens are often located in trees, including hollow logs and stumps. Raccoons also den in muskrat dwellings, woodchuck burrows, caves, mines, and barns.

In urban areas, the raccoon is happy to make its home in a city park, a ball field, or a backyard. Human-made structures such as sewers, garages, attics, and abandoned homes also provide shelter for denning.

In Germany, some raccoons escaped from fur farms. Others escaped from homes where they were kept as pets.

NOSE TO TAIL

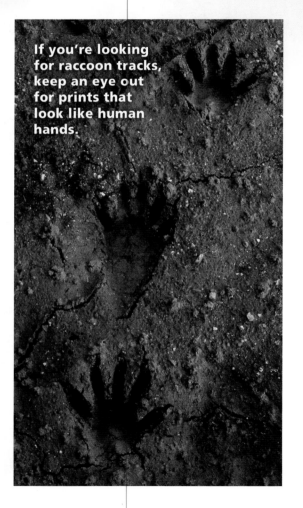

If you're looking for raccoon tracks, keep an eye out for prints that look like human hands.

Raccoons are medium-sized mammals with thick bodies and long, bushy tails. Northern raccoons are the largest raccoon species. This species ranges from 24 to 37 inches (60 to 95 cm) in length. It weighs 4 to 23 pounds (2 to 10 kg).

One of the raccoon's most notable features is its paws. There is no fur on the bottom of the paws. And, each toe ends in a sharp claw.

The five long, flexible toes on each forepaw act like fingers. Raccoons use these nimble toes to grasp food and to open containers.

A raccoon's forepaws are useful for opening garbage cans, doors, and more!

SIZE & SPECIES

Crab-eating raccoons are slightly smaller and narrower than their northern cousins.

The northern raccoon is well known for the special patterns of its fur. The tail has 4 to 10 rings. These alternate between black fur and cream to orange fur.

Raccoons have dark fur around the eyes. This dark fur is outlined with pale gray. So, a raccoon appears to be wearing a mask! The raccoon's broad head features a pointy nose and black eyes. The ears stand straight up and are about 1.5 inches (3.8 cm) tall.

The northern raccoon's coat has two layers. A dense **undercoat** protects the animal from cold temperatures. It makes up nearly 90 percent of the raccoon's **pelage**. The northern raccoon's coarse outer coat is black or iron-gray with brown. It appears grizzled, or salt-and-pepper.

The raccoon's coat is not waterproof. So, it gets heavy when wet. Raccoons are good swimmers. But they don't swim any farther than necessary.

Size and color vary by region. Common raccoons in the north are larger than those in the south. And, those in the north have more brown or blond fur, while silvery fur is more common in the south.

TELLING TAILS
The northern raccoon's tail makes up 60 percent of its length.

THE RACCOON

EARS

EYE

NOSE

PAW

TAIL

OMNIVORES

What does the raccoon like to eat? Many people would answer this question with one word, garbage! The raccoon is well known for its midnight raids on garbage cans, pet food, and anything else it can get its paws on.

In reality, the raccoon eats much more than that. Raccoons are **omnivorous**. In agricultural areas, they will dine on grains such as corn. In tropical regions, they feast on fresh fruit. Raccoons also like vegetables, nuts, and seeds.

Living near water means raccoons can enjoy fish, frogs, and crabs. They also eat grasshoppers, grubs, mice, squirrels, and even pheasants. And as good climbers, raccoons will steal birds' eggs for a tasty treat.

Raccoons have adapted to living near people and will take advantage of any available food source.

When heading out to eat, a raccoon travels in a straight line from its den to its food source.

AWAKE ALL NIGHT

Raccoons are **nocturnal**. They seldom venture out in the daytime. However when they do, it might be on a mild winter day. Food is harder to find at these times, so they must spend more time searching.

Each night, a raccoon might travel up to 1.5 miles (2.5 km) in search of food. In summer, more food is available in a smaller area. In winter, raccoons have to travel farther to find enough food.

Before the colder months, raccoons start eating more food. Their bodies store more fat, which helps them get ready for winter. Raccoons do not **hibernate**. Rather, raccoons rest for longer periods of time. They burn up to 50 percent of their body weight to stay alive during the winter.

When not resting, raccoons spend most of their time on the ground. They often move their bodies with shuffling steps. Despite this awkward **gait**, the raccoon can run up to 15 miles per hour (24 km/h)!

Raccoons are excellent climbers. They are specially adapted to do this. Sharp claws aid in scaling trees and other objects forward, backward, and even facedown.

A raccoon looks hunched over because its back legs are longer than its front legs.

DO A 180

A raccoon's feet rotate backward, so they don't have to climb down trees tail first.

ALONE, SOMETIMES

Many woodland animals, such as squirrels, rabbits, and bears, are solitary in nature. Others live in groups or close-knit families. Raccoons fall somewhere between solitary animals and those that remain in social groups.

Raccoons are usually alone. For example, mature males are quite solitary. On the other hand, young raccoons stay in their mother's den or small territory.

When food is scarce in winter, a couple of raccoons may show up at a feeding site together. These raccoons may or may not be related. If there is abundant food in one location, raccoons may **forage** there together.

A raccoon often has its own den. But, up to 20 raccoons may share a den. Usually, raccoons change their den site every few days. A mother and her young babies change den sites less often.

Raccoons are intelligent problem solvers. They can remember solutions to tasks for several years.

EYES IN THE NIGHT

Who do those shining eyes belong to? If they're yellow, they may belong to a raccoon.

SENSES & SOUNDS

Raccoons often look for food near water, which is why people once believed they washed their food before eating.

When raccoons are together, they communicate using their voices. Raccoons express their feelings with different sounds. These include purring, chittering, growling, snarling, and snorting. Raccoons also hiss, whistle, and scream. Humans who encounter raccoons may hear some of these sounds!

Raccoons also have excellent hearing and vision. Strange noises put the raccoon on guard. Special night vision helps them detect dangers. Lastly, the raccoon uses touch as a form of perception.

The raccoon's paws are highly sensitive. Raccoons use this sense to figure out such things as what kind of food they are holding. Scientists believe the raccoon's habit of dunking its food in water allows it to understand what it is holding. It not only softens the food, it helps raccoons pick out foreign objects.

Baby raccoons whine for food and attention! Mothers also use special trills to communicate with their young.

BABY RACCOONS

Tiny newborn raccoon kits rely completely on their mother.

Northern raccoons generally reproduce one time per year. Mating season is in spring, from January to June. Raccoons living in the southeastern United States mate later than those in other parts of the common raccoon's range. During this time, the male raccoon increases its range in order to find its mate. Male and female raccoons occasionally share a den while breeding.

The female common raccoon is **pregnant** for 63 to 65 days. Then, she gives birth to two to seven baby raccoons, or kits. The average **litter** size is four.

Raccoons are born with their eyes sealed shut. Their bodies are covered in fur that is darker than the fur of older raccoons. And, the helpless kits weigh just a few ounces.

Only raccoon mothers care for their kits. Fathers do not help.

Luckily, the mother raccoon stays close to care for her young. She will attack predators to protect them. The tiny kits can see 18 to 24 days after birth. By 7 weeks of age, young raccoons can walk, run, climb, and change dens.

By 8 to 10 weeks of age, kits tag along with their mother for **foraging**. They finish **weaning** around this same time. They watch their mother to learn how to eat a wide range of foods. Despite their new ability to find their own food, many young raccoons remain close to their family. Newly independent raccoons often den in their mother's home range and near her den.

Females will be ready to reproduce at 1 year of age. Males reach this stage at 2 years of age. However, most raccoons die before 2 years of age. Wild raccoons surviving past their second birthday live up to 16 years. Raccoons in captivity live up to 21 years.

Young raccoons spend time with their littermates until they go off on their own.

BOYS & GIRLS

A male raccoon is called a boar.
A female is called a sow.

ENEMIES & DEFENSES

Why do so few raccoons live past age two? Young raccoons face many dangers in their vulnerable state. For example, snakes and ravens attack young raccoons.

Adult raccoons also must defend against enemies. Predators from the air, such as hawks and great horned owls, prey on raccoons. Larger predators, including coyotes, wolves, bobcats, and cougars, seek raccoons for a tasty meal. Red foxes, fishers, and **domestic** dogs are also a threat.

The raccoon's best defense against predators is to be invisible. Staying in its den, quiet and watchful during the day, reduces the raccoon's chances of being noticed by predators.

If a raccoon is spotted, its next best defense is to run, climb, and hide! The raccoon's impressive climbing skills come in handy here. If all else fails and a raccoon is cornered, it can be **aggressive**. It uses its sharp claws and teeth to scratch and bite.

A raccoon's claws are important for defense, both for climbing and for scratching. They are nonretractile, which means they are always out.

RACCOONS & HUMANS

The raccoon faces other challenges as well. Several diseases cause raccoons to become seriously ill. These include distemper, trichinosis, and roundworm infection. Many raccoons are also infected by rabies, which is fatal to humans and pets if left untreated.

In addition, raccoons can harm farm field, orchard, and vineyard crops. Some people keep raccoons as pets, but this is illegal in many states. Adult raccoons can be especially destructive, as well as dangerous.

Humans also pose a threat to the raccoon population. Raccoon hunting and trapping for food and fur has taken place for many generations. Today, raccoons are also killed by cars and poisons.

Despite their many challenges, northern raccoons are far from extinction. The raccoon population is growing! Why? There are many raccoons to reproduce. In addition, the raccoon's ability to adapt to change keeps the population strong. They will be a common sight in neighborhoods for years to come.

THE NEW WORLD
The first known mention of raccoons in writing is from Christopher Columbus.

Scientists believe raccoons are smarter than house cats.

GLOSSARY

aggressive (uh-GREH-sihv) - displaying hostility.

domestic - tame, especially relating to animals.

endangered - in danger of becoming extinct.

evolve - to develop gradually.

forage - to search.

gait - the manner of walking or running.

habitat - a place where a living thing is naturally found.

hemisphere - one half of Earth.

hibernate - to spend a period of time, such as the winter, in deep sleep.

litter - all of the kits born to a mother raccoon at one time.

nocturnal - active at night.

nuisance (NOO-suhnts) - something that is annoying or causes trouble.

omnivorous - eating both plants and animals.

pelage (PEH-lihj) - the hairy covering of a mammal.

pregnant - having one or more babies growing within the body.

undercoat - short hair or fur partly covered by longer protective fur.

urban - of or relating to a city.

wean - to accustom an animal to food other than its mother's milk.

WEBSITES

To learn more about Backyard Animals,
visit **booklinks.abdopublishing.com**. These links are routinely
monitored and updated to provide the most current information available.

INDEX